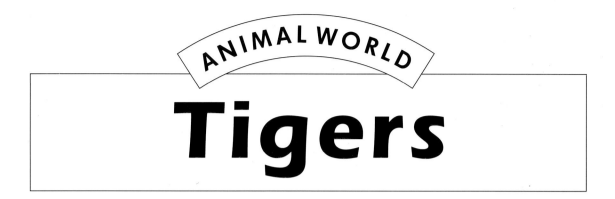

Tiger
ANIMAL WORLD

Written by Jenny Wood

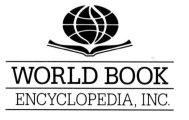

WORLD BOOK
ENCYCLOPEDIA, INC.

A SCOTT FETZER COMPANY

Copyright © 1991 Merlion Publishing Ltd

Published by World Book, Inc.
525 West Monroe Street
Chicago IL 60661
USA

Printed in Singapore by Kim Hup Lee

ISBN 0-7166-3304-3

A/IA

Design: Ann Samuel
Subject Consultant: Dr Julian Hector, Lecturer in Zoology, Anglia Polytechnic, Cambridge, UK

Illustration credits:
Lynda Arnold/Linden Artists Ltd: pages 16/17
Richard Berridge: cover background
Kim Blundell/John Martin & Artists Ltd: pages 15, 16 (top), 24/25 (bottom), 27 (top), 33, 39
Derek Bown/Linden Artists Ltd: pages 6/7, 22/23, 37
Maggie Brand/Maggie Mundy: pages 12/13, 18, 20/21, 28/29, 40/41
Nina O'Connell/B L Kearley Ltd: pages 9, 30/31
David Palmer/Temple Rogers: pages 26/27, 34/35
Peter Visscher: pages 10/11, 24/25

Photographic credits:
Bruce Coleman Ltd: pages 12 (Günter Ziesler), 42 (Alain Compost)
Frank Lane Picture Agency Ltd: pages 8, 14/15, 36 (Terry Whittaker), 43 (Philip Perry)
NHPA: pages 38/39 (Gerard Lacz)
Oxford Scientific Films: cover (Belinda Wright)
Silvestris/Frank Lane Picture Agency Ltd: pages 18/19, 28, 32/33

Contents

Let's look at tigers   6

Different kinds of tiger   8

Do tigers live near you?   10

Where do tigers live?   12

Do tigers talk?   14

How do tigers move?   16

Where do tigers sleep?   18

What do tigers eat?   20

How do tigers find food?   22

How does a tiger catch its prey?   24

Inside story   26

How do tigers keep safe?   28

Are tigers ever in danger?   30

How do tigers find a mate?   32

A new life   34

What do young tigers look like?   36

What do young tigers eat?   38

How do young tigers learn?   40

Tigers in danger   42

Glossary   44

Tiger Quiz   45

Index   47

Let's look at tigers

Tigers are the largest, strongest, and fiercest members of the cat family. They hunt and kill other animals for food.

Tigers can run fast. They can also jump, swim, and climb trees. They have sharp teeth and claws, as well as good eyesight and hearing. A tiger's body is perfectly designed for life as a hunter.

A tiger can hear sound from many different directions.

Tigers can see well in the dark. The whole of the inside surface of each eye is like a mirror, that lets in as much light as possible.

A tiger can feel things with its whiskers.

Sharp teeth for piercing and tearing at the flesh of prey.

Sharp claws for catching and holding onto prey.

All tigers have striped coats, but different kinds of tiger have different colors of fur.

Strong back and leg muscles.

A tiger's back legs are longer than its front legs, to make jumping easy.

Soft pads of skin on a tiger's paws allow it to prowl silently through the forest.

Different kinds of tiger

The large Siberian tiger lives farther north than any other tiger. Its thick coat keeps it warm during the cold winters.

There are seven kinds of tiger alive today. Three of these, the Caspian tiger, the South Chinese tiger, and the Javan tiger, may soon become extinct because there are so few of them left in the wild.

Each of the remaining four kinds of tiger looks slightly different.

How many tigers are left?

The Siberian tiger
The largest of all tigers. About 300 live in the wild.

The Bengal tiger
The best-known tiger. About 3,000 live in the wild.

The Indo-Chinese tiger
No one knows exactly how many of these tigers live in the wild.

The Sumatran tiger
The smallest of all tigers. Only a few hundred live in the wild.

Do tigers live near you?

If you live in one of the countries named on the map, the answer is "Yes"! All wild tigers are found in Asia. Some survive in the cold, snow-covered pine forests of Siberia. Others live in the hot, steamy tropical rain forests of Sumatra. But most stalk the grassy jungles of Northern India.

 Bengal tiger
India, Bhutan, Sikkim,
Nepal, Bangladesh

Indo-Chinese tiger
China, Burma, Laos,
Vietnam, Thailand,
Cambodia, Malaysia

 Sumatran tiger
Sumatra

Siberian tiger
Siberia

Siberia

China

Sikkim   Bhutan
Nepal

Bangladesh

India   Burma

Laos

Thailand   Vietnam
Cambodia

Malaysia

Sumatra

Where do tigers live?

A tiger's natural habitat is forest country. As long as they have food, water, and somewhere to hide, tigers can survive.

Most tigers live alone. Each tiger has its own territory, or "home range," an area of forest where it lives and hunts. A male tiger's territory is always larger than that of a female. Both male and female tigers mark the edges of their territories by spraying urine and rubbing other scents on trees, bushes, and rocks. These smells tell other tigers to keep out.

This tiger is marking its territory by spraying urine onto a rock.

Tigers live in all types of forest.

Do tigers talk?

Tigers don't talk by using words as we do, but they make sounds that mean something to other tigers and to other animals. They use facial expressions, too, to pass messages. Even the way a tiger moves its tail may be important!

Tigers hate being disturbed when they are eating. If another animal approaches, the tiger gives a warning growl. It then opens its mouth and pulls back its lips to show its teeth. It flattens its ears, narrows its eyes, and snarls. Its tail twitches from side to side. The tiger's message to the intruder is – GO AWAY OR I'LL ATTACK!

15

Did you know?

Tigers are superb swimmers, and often swim across rivers in search of prey. On hot days, they plunge into the water to cool down.

How do tigers move?

Tigers move gracefully and smoothly. The soft pads on their feet help them to walk almost silently. When they walk, tigers move both their left legs forward, then both their right legs. To speed up, a tiger pushes off from its hind legs and bounds away, covering about four yards with every bound. When it pounces on its prey, a tiger may make a giant leap of about six-and-a-half yards.

Where do tigers sleep?

Tigers hunt at night, so they spend most of each day dozing. A tiger will rest in a cool, shady patch on the forest floor, or among long grass.

Tigers often sleep, too, after they have eaten. When their stomachs are full, they find it more difficult to move around, so they sleep until the food has been digested.

Sometimes a tiger will sleep stretched out along the branch of a tree.

What do tigers eat?

Tigers are carnivores, which means that they eat meat. A tiger's favorite meal is a deer, wild pig, or antelope, but it will also attack a buffalo, wild ox, young elephant, or monkey. Tigers that live near farms sometimes eat sheep, cattle, and goats from the farmers' herds.

A tiger may take several hours or even days to find food and make a kill. Although tigers can run fast, they do so only over short distances. If they do not catch their prey quickly, they soon give up because they get tired very easily. So it may take up to 20 tries before a tiger finally manages to catch a meal! If desperate for food, a tiger will make do with a frog or small bird.

Bird

Frog

Monkey

Elephant calf

20

Wild pig

Sambar (a type of deer)

Buffalo

Antelope

Wild ox

21

How do tigers find food?

Tigers are very skillful hunters. Their eyes, ears, and even their whiskers help them to track down prey in the twilight.

Eyes

A tiger's eyes face forward. This allows the tiger to see objects ahead of it, and to the side. The tiger can also judge how far away an object is, which is very important when it is about to pounce on its prey.

In dim light, the pupils of a tiger's eyes become larger, to let in as much light as possible.

Ears

A tiger has 30 muscles in each of its ears (we have only six), which help it hear clearly. The tiger moves its ear flaps backward and forward, to find out exactly where a sound is coming from.

Whiskers

Tigers use their long, stiff whiskers to feel objects they cannot see clearly.

How does a tiger catch its prey?

At dusk the tiger moves softly through the long grass, in search of a meal. Its eyes and ears are alert for the slightest movement or sound. It soon catches sight of a deer standing by a water-hole. Slowly and silently, the tiger pads toward its prey, taking care to stay downwind so that the deer cannot smell it approaching. It crouches in the reeds near the water's edge, and waits.

Suddenly the tiger leaps out from its hiding place. It stuns the deer with a blow from its front paws then sinks its teeth into the deer's neck and squeezes hard. The hunt is over.

Did you know?

A tiger has two very large upper front teeth, or fang teeth, which it uses for grabbing and biting its victim.

A tiger's claws are normally pulled back inside folds of skin between the toes. But when a tiger attacks, its claws are pushed forward to help the animal hold firmly onto its prey.

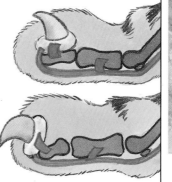

Inside story

An adult tiger needs to eat about 33 pounds of meat every day in order to survive. But it may eat as much as 75 pounds of meat in one night! The carcass of a large animal such as a deer or antelope will provide a tiger with food for several days.

A tiger always drags the dead body of its prey into the undergrowth before starting to eat.

The tiger uses its small front teeth, called incisors, as well as its claws to tear off the animal's skin and uncover the layer of meat underneath.

A male tiger will try to make a kill every seven or eight days. A female tiger with cubs needs to kill every five or six days because she has extra mouths to feed.

The tiger uses its side teeth to slice off chunks of meat from the carcass. A tiger's teeth are not designed for chewing, so the animal just swallows the lumps of meat whole.

When the tiger has eaten enough, it hides the carcass under a pile of grass or earth. It returns each day until every scrap has been eaten.

27

How do tigers keep safe?

Tigers keep safe by being difficult to find. In fact, trying to spot a tiger in the wild is like playing hide and seek! The stripes on a tiger's fur seem to make the animal disappear among the long grasses, leafy branches, and patchy sunlight of its forest home. This kind of disguise is known as camouflage.

Tigers are safe, too, because they are fierce and powerful. Most other animals stay well away.

This Bengal tiger is creeping through long grass in search of prey.

How many tigers can you spot in this picture?

Are tigers ever in danger?

Tigers are sometimes wounded by animals such as porcupines and cobras, but they are rarely attacked. Female tigers may be threatened by other animals such as wild dogs, but the dogs are usually after the tiger's food, not the tiger herself.

If a king cobra is stepped on by a tiger, it will strike. The king cobra is one of the most dangerous snakes in the world. It can grow up to six-and-a-half yards long and its venom can kill a human in 15 minutes!

Wild dogs sometimes menace female tigers, in an attempt to drive them away from their food. These dogs are extremely fierce and hunt in large packs.

When a tiger goes down to the water to drink, it must beware of crocodiles. A crocodile may pull a tiger into the river then hold it underwater until it drowns.

When attacked, a porcupine backs into its attacker, stabbing its sharp quills into the creature's skin. The quills are very difficult to remove, so tigers try to avoid contact with porcupines if they can!

How do tigers find a mate?

When a male tiger enters a female's home range, he can tell by the scent markings she has left on the trees and bushes whether or not she is ready to mate. If she is, then the male approaches her. The two animals snarl and growl at first, but then rub heads and lick each other before mating. The male stays with the female for a few days before wandering off through the forest in search of another partner.

Tigers are ready to breed when they are three or four years old.

Did you know?

There are only two or three days during each breeding season when a female tiger is willing to mate.

Sometimes, after mating, the female jumps up and cuffs the male on the face!

Males sometimes fight for the chance to mate with a female. The loser skulks away into the forest.

33

A new life

Tiger cubs grow inside their mother for about 15 weeks before they are born. The mother looks for a safe, comfortable place in which to give birth. She may find a cave or a hollow tree trunk, or she may make a soft nest of grass and leaves in the forest.

A female tiger usually carries two or three cubs at the same time.

What do young tigers look like?

A tiger cub's fur is often light in color. The fur and stripes begin to darken when the cub is about four months old.

Like all cats, tigers are born blind and helpless. Their mother keeps them safe, and gives them food. The cubs soon open their eyes and begin to move around, but they still have a lot to learn and will stay with their mother for about two years.

Birth
Newborn cubs are blind and helpless. Each one measures about 24 inches from its head to the tip of its tail, and weighs between two and four pounds.

2 weeks
The cubs begin to grow their first set of teeth.

3 weeks
The cubs can see clearly by the time they are three weeks old.

6 weeks
The cubs are ready to go with their mother when she hunts.

1 year
The cubs begin to learn to hunt for themselves.

2 years
The cubs are now old enough and strong enough to look after themselves.

What do young tigers eat?

At first, tiger cubs feed only on their mother's milk. The milk contains all the proteins, fats, sugars, and vitamins that the young cubs need to help them grow. From the age of three months, the cubs also begin to eat small amounts of meat which their mother finds for them. As they get older, their mother teaches them to eat more meat and drink less milk, until they stop drinking her milk altogether.

Tiger cubs sucking milk from their mother's nipples.

Mother tigers try to get their cubs to eat meat – but they probably don't give the cubs steaks!

How do young tigers learn?

The mother tiger teaches her cubs how to hunt and how to look after themselves in the wild. The father does not help at all.

At first, the mother tiger kills animals for her cubs to eat. She leaves them in a safe place each time she goes off to hunt. But soon the cubs are old enough to go with her, and they watch how she hunts her prey and then kills it. The first animal a tiger cub kills by itself may be a small wild pig.

Tiger cubs learn through play, too.

Tigers in danger

In recent years, tigers have had to struggle to survive. In most countries where tigers live, it is now against the law to kill them, but people still hunt tigers for sport and for their skins.

Tigers have lost much of their habitat, too. The number of people in the world is getting larger all the time, and so more and more land is needed for housing and for growing food. Huge areas of the forests in which tigers live have been cleared for farmland. Many tigers have died because they have nowhere to live and no food to eat.

This tiger skin is being stretched out to dry before being put on sale in a souvenir shop.

Tigers are kept in many of the world's zoos. The zoos try to breed the tigers so that they can release the young back into the wild.

Tiger Quiz — answers

1   You could choose from the following kinds of tiger: Caspian, South Chinese, Javan, Siberian, Bengal, Indo-Chinese, Sumatran.

2   The country with the most tigers is India.

3   Other countries where tigers live are Sikkim, Bhutan, Siberia, China, Nepal, Bangladesh, Burma, Laos, Thailand, Cambodia, Vietnam, Malaysia, Sumatra.

4   The tiger that lives the farthest north is the Siberian tiger.

5   Yes, tigers can swim very well.

6   The farthest a tiger can leap is about six and a half yards (six meters).

7   Tigers hunt at night.

8   These are some of the things that tigers eat: elephant calves, frogs, monkeys, birds, wild pigs, wild oxen, antelope, sambar, buffalo.

9   A tiger has 30 muscles in each ear.

10 A tiger needs to eat about 33 pounds (15 kilograms) of meat every day.

11 A tiger's stripes are useful as camouflage.

12 A tiger mother usually has two or three cubs in each litter.

13 No, a male tiger does not help bring up his cubs.

Index

antelope   20, 21, 26
Asia   10

baby tiger see cub
Bangladesh   10, 11
Bengal tiger   9, 10, 28
Bhutan   10, 11
bird   20
birth   34, 37
body   6–7, 34–35
   keeping cool   16
buffalo   20, 21
Burma   10, 11

Cambodia   10, 11
camouflage   28–29, 44
carnivore   20, 44
Caspian tiger   9
cat   6, 37
China   10, 11
claw   6, 25, 26
climbing   6
coat see fur
cobra   30
communication   14–15
crocodile   31
cub   34–35, 37, 40–41, 44
   food   38–39, 40
   fur   36, 37
   size   37

deer   20, 21, 24, 26
drinking   38–39

ear   6, 23
eating   15, 18, 20, 26–27
   cub   38–39
elephant   20

enemies   30–31
   human   43
eye   6, 22
   see also sight

face   14–15
   whiskers   6, 22, 23
fang   24
female tiger   12, 30, 32–33
   mother   27, 34–35, 37, 38–39,
food   6, 20–21, 26–27
   cub's   38–39, 40
   see also prey
foot   6, 7, 17, 25
frog   20
fur   7, 8, 9, 28
   cub's   36, 37

habitat   9, 10, 12, 13, 44
   destruction of   43
hearing   6, 23
hunting   18, 20, 24–25
   cub   37, 40
   finding prey   22–23

incisor   26
India   10, 11
Indo-Chinese tiger   9, 10

Javan tiger   9

king cobra   30

Laos   10, 11
leg   7, 17

Malaysia   10, 11
male tiger   12, 27, 32–33, 40

mating   32–33, 44
milk   38–39
monkey   20
mother   27, 34–35, 37, 38–39
  teaching cubs   37, 39, 40
movement   6, 7, 17
  climbing   6
  running   6, 17, 20
  swimming   6, 16
  walking   17
muscle   7, 23

Nepal   10, 11
noise   15

paw   7, 25
population   9
porcupine   30, 31
prey   20–21, 24, 40, 44
  catching   6, 17, 20, 22, 24–25

sambar   21
scent   12, 33, 44
senses   6, 12, 22–23, 37
Siberia   10, 11
Siberian tiger   8, 9, 10
sight   6, 22, 37
Sikkim   10, 11
skin   42–43, 44
  fur   7, 8, 9, 28
sleep   18–19
smell   12
South Chinese tiger   9
Sumatra   10, 11
Sumatran tiger   9, 10
swimming   6, 16

tail   15
teeth   6, 24, 26, 27
  cub's   37
territory   12, 44
Thailand   10, 11

tiger
  kinds of   9
  size (cub)   37
  where they live   9, 10–11, 12–13
tropical rainforest   10, 44

urine   12

venom   30
Vietnam   10, 11

walking   17
whisker   6, 22, 23
wild dog   30
wild ox   20, 21
wild pig   20, 21, 40
world map   10–11

young tiger see **cub**

zoo   43